حجاب چرخان

The Swirling Hijaab

Na'ima bint Robert
Nilesh Mistry

Farsi Translation by Parisima Ahmadi-Ziabari

mantra lingua

حجاب مادر من سیاه و نرم و گشاد است،

My mum's hijaab is black and soft
and wide,

یک قلعه است که میتوانم در آن پنهان شوم!

A fort for me to hide inside!

بادبان یک کشتی است، که در
هوا تکان می خورد،

A ship's sails flapping in the air,

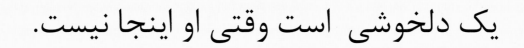

یک دلخوشی است وقتی او اینجا نیست.

A comforter when she's not there.

یک چادر بدوی،

A bedouin tent,

یک ساری عروسی،

A wedding sari,

یک پارچه برای میهمانی عصرانهٔ من است.

A cloth for my tea party.

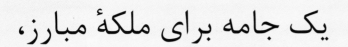

یک جامه برای ملکهٔ مبارز،

A warrior queen's cloak,

یک بار سفر برای خانه بدوش،

A nomad's baggage,

یک پتو برای وقتی که احتیاج به استراحت دارم!

A blanket when I need a rest!

امّا بهترین کاری که حجاب می‌کند
پوشش
مادرم در همراهی کردن با ایمان
او است.

But covering my mum
as part of her faith
Is what the hijaab does best.

Bismillahir-Rahmanir-Raheem

For the daughters of Islam, past, present and future

N.B.R.

For Saarah, Farheen & Rayaan

N.M.

 The Swirling Hijaab is one of many sound enabled books.
Touch the circle with TalkingPEN for a list of the other titles.

First published in 2002 Mantra Lingua Ltd
Global House, 303 Ballards Lane, London N12 8NP
www.mantralingua.com

Text copyright © 2002 Na'ima bint Robert
Illustrations copyright © 2002 Nilesh Mistry
Dual language text copyright © 2002 Mantra Lingua
Audio copyright © 2008 Mantra Lingua
All rights reserved

A CIP record for this book is available from the British Library